Presented to _____

From _____

BY HELEN STEINER RICE

HELEN STEINER RICE

Heart Gifts

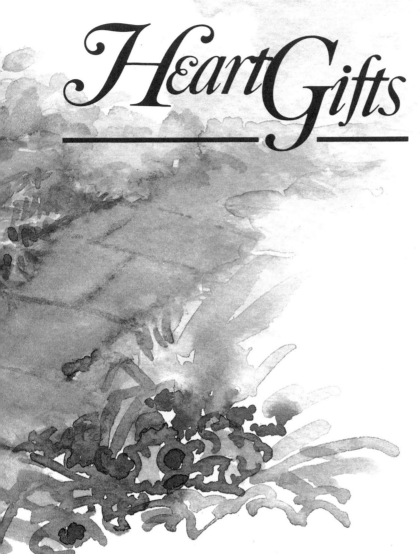

Fleming H. Revell Company
Old Tappan, New Jersey

ISBN 0-8007-1520-9
Interior illustrations Copyright © 1987 by Steffi Karen Rubin.
Text copyright © 1968 by Fleming H. Revell Company, 1987 by the
Helen Steiner Rice Foundation
Old Tappan, New Jersey 07675
Library of Congress Catalog Card Number: 68-28438
Printed in the United States of America

FOREWORD

Show me the way,
        not to fortune and fame,
Not how to win laurels
        or praise for my name—
But show me the way
        to spread "the Great Story"
That "Thine is the Kingdom
        and Power and Glory."

HELEN STEINER RICE

CONTENTS

INTRODUCTION

When we first began publishing the poetry of Helen Steiner Rice, we started with a small collection of verse, handpicked by Helen herself. She titled it *Heart Gifts*, for that's what they were: small gifts of poetry from her heart, written to speak to the hearts of her readers.

Published nearly twenty years ago, *Heart Gifts* has touched hundreds of thousands of lives. We have since published many other collections of Helen's poetry which have had the same enthusiastic welcome that *Heart Gifts* has. In fact, her poetry is so well loved around the world that she came to be known as the "poet laureate of popular verse."

How could one tiny woman make such a profound impact on so many people?

One observer said she had "the rare gift of sensing people's fundamental needs, of reaching into their hearts and leaving there a firmer grasp of the lasting realities of faith and hope and love." But she was not satisfied to simply let this gift go undeveloped. Her gifts of insight and wisdom were nurtured by her continual interaction with people in need. She developed long-lasting relationships with the people who responded to her poetry: the heartbroken, the ill, the lonely, and the needy, as well as the rejoicing and hope-filled.

Helen Steiner Rice gloried in the ordinary. She knew that the people who have the best grasp on life are those who most would call common or ordinary, not the "upwardly mobile" or the "movers and shakers." No, those who truly understand the ebb and flow of life are those who struggle with the day-to-day joys and disappointments of jobs and families. Those who rejoice in a baby's first step, a grandchild's crayon picture, a daughter's wedding. Those who weep for a father's death or sister's illness. Those who count among their most treasured possessions the memories of family and friends.

And these are the folks Helen Steiner Rice valued. She sought their company, listened to their laughter, shared their tears. And when she wrote, she wrote for them, giving voice to their thoughts and feelings.

As we began to plan this reissue of *Heart Gifts*, we were struck again with the timelessness of Helen's verse. Her pen was stilled on April 23, 1981, but her words continue to offer comfort and hope to a needy world. And her prayer for peace is as appropriate today as the day she wrote it.

God of Love—Forgive! Forgive!
Teach us how to Truly Live. . . .
And someday may men realize
That all the earth, the seas, the skies
Belong to God who made us all,
The rich, the poor, the great, the small,
And in the Father's Holy Sight
No man is yellow, black, or white,
And Peace on Earth cannot be found
Until we meet on Common Ground
And every man becomes a Brother
Who worships God and loves all others

As you read through this volume, first her poems, then
her story, "Out of My Life," we hope that you will be re-
newed, refreshed, and encouraged.

The Publishers

HeartGifts

"Heart Gifts"

It's not the things that can be bought
    that are life's richest treasure,
It's just the little "heart gifts"
    that money cannot measure . . .
A cheerful smile, a friendly word,
    a sympathetic nod
Are priceless little treasures
    from the storehouse of our God . . .
They are the things that can't be bought
    with silver or with gold,
For thoughtfulness and kindness
    and love are never sold . . .
They are the priceless things in life
    for which no one can pay,
And the giver finds rich recompense
    in *giving them away.*

A Sure Way to a Happy Day

Happiness is something
      we create in our mind,
It's not something you search for
      and so seldom find—
It's just waking up
      and beginning the day
By counting our blessings
      and kneeling to pray—
It's giving up thoughts
      that breed discontent
And accepting what comes
      as a "gift heaven-sent"—
It's giving up wishing
      for things we have not
And making the best of
      whatever we've got—
It's knowing that life
      is determined for us,
And pursuing our tasks
      without fret, fume, or fuss—
For it's by completing
      what God gives us to do
That we find real contentment
      and happiness, too.

Prayers Are the Stairs to God

Prayers are the stairs
We must climb every day,
If we would reach God
There is no other way,
For we learn to know God
When we meet Him in prayer
And ask Him to lighten
Our burden of care—
So start in the morning
And, though the way's steep,
Climb ever upward
'Til your eyes close in sleep—
For prayers are the stairs
That lead to the Lord,
And to meet Him in prayer
Is the climber's reward.

There's Sunshine in a Smile

Life is a mixture
     of sunshine and rain,
Laughter and pleasure,
     teardrops and pain,
All days can't be bright,
     but it's certainly true,
There was never a cloud
     the sun didn't shine through—
So just keep on smiling
     whatever betide you,
Secure in the knowledge
     God is always beside you,
And you'll find when you smile
     your day will be brighter
And all of your burdens
     will seem so much lighter—
For each time you smile
     you will find it is true
Somebody, somewhere
     will *smile back at you,*
And nothing on earth
     can make life more worthwhile
Than the sunshine and warmth
     of a *beautiful smile.*

Widen My Vision

God, open my eyes
     so I may see
And feel Your presence
     close to me . . .
Give me strength
     for my stumbling feet
As I battle the crowd
     on life's busy street,
And widen the vision
     of my unseeing eyes
So in passing faces
     I'll recognize
Not just a stranger,
     unloved and unknown,
But a friend with a heart
     that is much like my own . . .
Give me perception
     to make me aware
That scattered profusely
     on life's thoroughfare
Are the best *Gifts of God*
     that we daily pass by
As we look at the world
     with an *unseeing eye*.

Anywhere Is a Place of Prayer If God Is There

I have prayed on my knees in the morning,
I have prayed as I walked along,
I have prayed in the silence and darkness
And I've prayed to the tune of a song—
I have prayed in the midst of triumph
And I've prayed when I suffered defeat,
I have prayed on the sands of the seashore
Where the waves of the ocean beat—
I have prayed in a velvet-hushed forest
Where the quietness calmed my fears,
I have prayed through suffering and heartache
When my eyes were blinded with tears—
I have prayed in churches and chapels,
Cathedrals and synagogues, too,
But often I've had the feeling
That my prayers were not getting through,
And I realized then that our Father
Is not really concerned *where* we pray
Or impressed by our manner of worship
Or the eloquent words that we say . . .
He is only concerned with our feelings,
And He looks deep into our heart
And hears the "cry of our soul's deep need"
That no words could ever impart . . .
So it isn't the prayer that's expressive
Or offered in some special spot,
It's the sincere plea of a sinner
And God can tell whether or not
We honestly seek His forgiveness
And earnestly mean what we say,
And then and then only He answers
The prayer that we fervently pray.

Where Can We Find Him?

Where can we find *the Holy One?*
Where can we see *His Only Son?*
The Wise Men asked, and we're asking still,
Where can we find this Man of Good Will?
Is He far away in some distant place,
Ruling unseen from His throne of grace?
Is there nothing on earth that man can see
To give him proof of *Eternity?*
It's true we have never looked on His face,
But His likeness shines forth from every place,
For *the Hand of God* is everywhere
Along life's busy thoroughfare . . .
And His presence can be felt and seen
Right in the midst of our daily routine,
The things we touch and see and feel
Are what makes God so very real . . .
The silent stars in timeless skies,
The wonderment in children's eyes,
The gossamer wings of a humming bird,
The joy that comes from a kindly word . . .
The autumn haze, the breath of spring,
The chirping song the crickets sing,
A rosebud in a slender vase,
A smile upon a friendly face . . .
In everything both great and small
We see *the Hand of God in All,*
And every day, somewhere, someplace,
We see *the Likeness of His Face . . .*

For who can watch a new day's birth
Or touch the warm, life-giving earth,
Or feel the softness of the breeze
Or look at skies through lacy trees
And say they've never seen His face
Or looked upon His throne of grace!

God Is Never Beyond Our Reach

No one ever sought the Father
And found *He* was not *there,*
And no burden is too heavy
To be lightened by a prayer,
No problem is too intricate
And no sorrow that we face
Is too deep and devastating
To be softened by His grace,
No trials and tribulations
Are beyond what we can bear
If we can share them with *Our Father*
As we talk to *Him* in prayer—
And men of every color,
Every race and every creed
Have but to seek the Father
In their deepest hour of need—
God asks for no credentials,
He accepts us with our flaws,
He is kind and understanding
And He welcomes us because
We are His erring children
And He loves us every one,
And He freely and completely
Forgives all that we have done,
Asking only if we're ready,
To follow *where He leads*—
Content that in His wisdom
He will answer all our needs.

God's Jewels

We watch the rich and famous
Bedecked in precious jewels,
Enjoying earthly pleasures,
Defying moral rules—
And in our mood of discontent
We sink into despair
And long for earthly riches
And feel cheated of our share—
But stop these idle musings,
God has stored up for you
Treasures that are far beyond
Earth's jewels and riches, too—
For never, never discount
What God has promised man
If he will walk in meekness
And accept God's flawless plan—
For if we heed His teachings
As we journey through the years,
We'll find the richest jewels of all
Are *crystalized* from *tears*.

The Peace of Meditation

So we may know God better
And feel His quiet power,
Let us daily keep in silence
A *meditation hour*—
For to understand God's greatness
And to use His gifts each day
The soul must learn to meet Him
In a meditative way,
For our Father tells His children
That if they would know His will
They must seek Him in the silence
When all is calm and still . . .
For nature's greatest forces
Are found in quiet things
Like softly falling snowflakes
Drifting down on angels' wings,
Or petals dropping soundlessly
From a lovely full-blown rose,
So God comes closest to us
When our souls are in repose . . .
So let us plan with prayerful care
To always allocate
A certain portion of each day
To be still and meditate . . .
For when everything is quiet
And we're lost in meditation,
Our soul is then preparing
For a deeper dedication
That will make it wholly possible
To quietly endure
The violent world around us—
For in God we are secure.

Thank God for Little Things

Thank You, God, for little things
      that often come our way—
The things we take for granted
      but don't mention when we pray—
The unexpected courtesy,
      the thoughtful, kindly deed—
A hand reached out to help us
      in the time of sudden need—
Oh, make us more aware, dear God,
      of little daily graces
That come to us with "sweet surprise"
      from never-dreamed-of places.

Quit Supposin'

Don't start your day by supposin'
  that trouble is just ahead,
It's better to stop supposin'
  and start with a prayer instead,
And make it a prayer of *Thanksgiving*
  for the wonderful things God has wrought
Like the beautiful sunrise and sunset,
  "God's Gifts" that are free
  and not bought—
For what is the use of supposin'
  the dire things that could happen to you
And worrying about some misfortune
  that seldom if ever comes true—
But instead of just idle supposin'
  step forward to meet each new day
Secure in the knowledge God's near you
  to lead you each step of the way—
For supposin' the worst things will happen
  only helps to make them come true
And you darken the bright, happy moments
  that the dear Lord has given to you—
So if you desire to be happy
  and get rid of the *"misery of dread"*
Just give up *"Supposin' the worst things"*
  and look for *"the best things"* instead.

In Hours of Discouragement
God Is Our Encouragement

Sometimes we feel uncertain
And unsure of everything,
Afraid to make decisions,
Dreading what the day will bring—
We keep wishing it were possible
To dispel all fear and doubt
And to understand more readily
Just what life is all about—
God has given us the answers
Which too often go unheeded,
But if we search His promises
We'll find everything that's needed
To lift our faltering spirits
And renew our courage, too,

For there's absolutely nothing
Too much for God to do—
For the Lord is our salvation
And our strength in every fight,
Our redeemer and protector,
Our eternal guiding light—
He has promised to sustain us,
He's our refuge from all harms,
And underneath this refuge
Are the everlasting arms—
So cast your burden on Him,
Seek His counsel when distressed,
And go to Him for comfort
When you're lonely and oppressed—
For God is our encouragement
In trouble and in trials,
And in suffering and in sorrow
He will turn our tears to smiles.

Never Borrow Sorrow From Tomorrow

Deal only with the present,
Never step into tomorrow,
For God asks us just to trust Him
And to never borrow sorrow—
For the future is not ours to know
And it may never be,
So let us live and give our best
And give it lavishly—
For to meet tomorrow's troubles
Before they are even ours
Is to anticipate the Saviour
And to doubt His all-wise powers—
So let us be content to solve
Our problems one by one,
Asking nothing of tomorrow
Except *"Thy Will be done."*

Trouble Is a Stepping-stone to Growth

Trouble is something no one can escape,
Everyone has it in some form or shape—
Some people hide it way down deep inside,
Some people bear it with gallant-like pride,
Some people worry and complain of their lot,
Some people covet what they haven't got,
While others rebel and become bitter and old
With hopes that are dead and hearts that are cold . . .
But the wise man accepts whatever God sends,
Willing to yield like a storm-tossed tree bends,
Knowing that God never makes a mistake,
So whatever He sends they are willing to take—
For trouble is part and parcel of life
And no man can grow without trouble and strife,
And the steep hills ahead and high mountain peaks
Afford man at last the peace that he seeks—
So blest are the people who learn to accept
The trouble men try to escape and reject,
For in *our acceptance*
        we're given great grace
And courage and faith and the strength to face
The daily troubles that come to us all
So we may learn to stand "straight and tall"—
For the grandeur of life is born of defeat
For in overcoming we make life complete.

Unaware, We Pass "Him" By

On life's busy thoroughfares
We meet with *angels* unawares—
But we are too busy to listen or hear,
Too busy to sense that God is near,
Too busy to stop and recognize
The grief that lies in another's eyes,
Too busy to offer to help or share,
Too busy to sympathize or care,
Too busy to do the *good things* we should,
Telling ourselves we would if we could . . .
But life is too swift and the pace is too great
And we dare not pause for we might be late
For our next appointment which means so much,
We are willing to brush off the Saviour's touch,
And we tell ourselves there will come a day
We will have more time to pause on our way . . .
But before we know it "life's sun has set"
And we've passed the Saviour but never met,
For hurrying along life's thoroughfare
We passed Him by and remained unaware
That within the *very sight of our eye,*
Unnoticed, the Son of God passed by.

When Trouble Comes and Things Go Wrong!

Let us go quietly to God
      when troubles come to us,
Let us never stop to whimper
      or complain and fret and fuss,
Let us hide "our thorns" in "roses"
      and our sighs in "golden song"
And "our crosses" in a "crown of smiles"
      whenever things go wrong . . .
For no one can really help us
      as our troubles we bemoan,
For *comfort, help,* and *inner peace*
      must come from God alone . . .
So do not tell your neighbor,
      your companion or your friend
In the hope that they can help you
      bring your troubles to an end . . .
For they, too, have their problems,
      they are burdened just like you,
So *take your cross to Jesus*
      and *He will see you through* . . .
And waste no time in crying
      on the shoulder of a friend
But go directly to the Lord
      for on Him you can depend . . .
For there's absolutely *nothing*
      that His mighty hand can't do
And He never is too busy
      to help and comfort you.

Fathers Are Wonderful People

Fathers are wonderful people
  too little understood,
And we do not sing their praises
  as often as we should . . .
For, somehow, Father seems to be
  the man who pays the bills,
While Mother binds up little hurts
  and nurses all our ills . . .
And Father struggles daily
  to live up to *"his image"*
As protector and provider
  and "hero of the scrimmage". . .
And perhaps that is the reason
  we sometimes get the notion
That Fathers are not subject
  to the thing we call emotion,
But if you look inside Dad's heart,
  where no one else can see,
You'll find he's sentimental
  and as "soft" as he can be . . .
But he's so busy every day
  in the grueling race of life,
He leaves the sentimental stuff
  to his partner and his wife . . .
But Fathers are just *wonderful*
  in a million different ways,
And they merit loving compliments
  and accolades of praise,

For the only reason Dad aspires
       to fortune and success
Is to make the family proud of him
       and to bring them happiness . . .
And like *our Heavenly Father,*
       he's a guardian and a guide,
Someone that we can count on
       to be *always on our side.*

A Tribute to All Daughters

Every home should have a daughter,
    for there's nothing like a girl
To keep the world around her
    in one continuous whirl . . .
From the moment she arrives on earth,
    and on through womanhood,
A daughter is a *female*
    who is seldom understood . . .
One minute she is laughing,
    the next she starts to cry,
Man just can't understand her
    and there's just no use to try . . .
She is soft and sweet and cuddly,
    but she's also wise and smart,
She's a wondrous combination
    of a mind and brain and heart . . .
And even in her baby days
    she's just a born coquette,
And anything she really wants
    she manages to get . . .
For even at a tender age
    she uses all her wiles
And she can melt the hardest heart
    with the sunshine of her smiles . . .
She starts out as a rosebud
    with her beauty unrevealed,
Then through a happy childhood
    her petals are unsealed . . .
She's soon a sweet girl graduate,
    and then a blushing bride,

And then a lovely woman
        as the rosebud opens wide . . .
And some day in the future,
        if it be God's gracious will,
She, too, will be a Mother
        and know that reverent thrill
That comes to every Mother
        whose heart is filled with love
When she beholds the "angel"
        that God sent her from above . . .
And there would be no life at all
        in this world or the other
Without a *darling daughter*
        who, in turn, becomes a *Mother!*

A Prayer for the Young and Lovely

Dear God, I keep praying
For the things I desire,
You tell me I'm selfish
And "playing with fire"—
It is hard to believe
I am selfish and vain,
My desires seem so real
And my needs seem so sane,
And yet You are wiser
And Your vision is wide
And You look down on me
And You see deep inside,
You know it's so easy
To change and distort,
And things that are evil
Seem so harmless a sport—
Oh, teach me, dear God,
To not rush ahead
But to pray for Your guidance
And to trust You instead,
For You know what I need

And that I'm only a slave
To the things that I want
And desire and crave—
Oh, God, in your mercy
Look down on me now
And see in my heart
That I love You somehow,
Although in my rashness,
Impatience and greed
I pray for the things
That I *want* and *don't need*—
And instead of a *crown*
Please send me a *cross*
And teach me to know
That *all gain* is but *loss,*
And show me the way
To joy without end,
With You as my *Father,*
Redeemer, and *Friend*—
And send me the things
That are hardest to bear,
And keep me forever
Safe in Thy care.

"This Too Will Pass Away"

If I can endure for this minute
Whatever is happening to me,
No matter how heavy my heart is
Or how "dark" the moment may be—
If I can remain calm and quiet
With all my world crashing about me,
Secure in the knowledge God loves me
When everyone else seems to doubt me—
If I can but keep on believing
What I know in my heart to be true,
That "darkness will fade with the morning"
And that *this will pass away, too*—
Then nothing in life can defeat me
For as long as this knowledge remains
I can suffer whatever is happening
For I know God will break "all the chains"
That are binding me tight in *"the Darkness"*
And trying to fill me with fear—
For there is *no night without dawning*
And I know that *"my morning"* is near.

More of Thee . . . Less of Me

Take me and break me and make me, dear God,
Just what You want me to be—
Give me the strength to accept what You send
And eyes with the vision to see
All the small arrogant ways that I have
And the vain little things that I do,
Make me aware that I'm often concerned
More with *myself* than with *You*,
Uncover before me my weakness and greed
And help me to search deep inside
So I may discover how easy it is
To be selfishly lost in my pride—
And then in Thy goodness and mercy
Look down on this weak, erring one
And tell me that I am forgiven
For all I've so willfully done,
And teach me to humbly start following
The path that the dear Saviour trod
So I'll find at the end of life's journey
"A Home in the city of God!"

Warm Our Hearts With Thy Love

Oh, God, who made the summer
    and warmed the earth with beauty,
Warm our hearts with gratitude
    and devotion to our duty,
For in this age of violence,
    rebellion and defiance
We've forgotten the true meaning
    of "dependable reliance"—
We have lost our sense of duty
    and our sense of values, too,
And what was once unsanctioned,
    no longer is taboo,
Our standards have been lowered
    and we resist all discipline,
And our vision has been narrowed
    and blinded to all sin—
Oh, put the summer brightness
    in our closed, unseeing eyes
So in the careworn faces
    that we pass we'll recognize
The heartbreak and the loneliness,
    the trouble and despair
That a word of understanding
    would make easier to bear—
Oh, God, look down on our cold hearts
    and warm them with Your love,
And grant us Your forgiveness
    which we're so unworthy of.

No Prayer Goes Unheard

Often we pause and wonder
When we kneel down to pray—
Can God really hear
The prayers that we say . . .
But if we keep praying
And talking to *Him*,
He'll brighten the soul
That was clouded and dim,
And as we continue
Our burden seems lighter,
Our sorrow is softened
And our outlook is brighter—
For though we feel helpless
And alone when we start,
Our prayer is the key
That opens the heart,
And as our heart opens
The dear Lord comes in
And the prayer that we felt
We could never begin
Is so easy to say
For the Lord understands
And gives us new strength
By the touch of His hands.

Daily Prayers Dissolve Your Cares

I meet God in the morning
And go with Him through the day,
Then in the stillness of the night
Before sleep comes I pray
That God will just "take over"
All the problems I couldn't solve
And in the peacefulness of sleep
My cares will all dissolve,
So when I open up my eyes
To greet another day
I'll find myself renewed in strength
And there'll open up a way
To meet what seemed impossible
For me to solve alone
And once again I'll be assured
I am never "*on my own*" . . .
For if we try to stand alone
We are weak and we will fall,

For God is always *Greatest*
When we're helpless, lost and small,
And no day is unmeetable
If on rising our first thought
Is to thank God for the blessings
That His loving care has brought . . .
For there can be no failures
Or hopeless, unsaved sinners
If we enlist the help of God
Who makes all losers winners . . .
So meet Him in the morning
And go with Him through the day
And thank Him for His guidance
Each evening when you pray,
And if you follow faithfully
This daily way to pray
You will never in your lifetime
Face another "hopeless day."

Before You Can Dry Another's
Tears—You Too Must Weep!

Let me not live a life that's free
From *"the things"* that draw me close to *Thee*—
For how can I ever hope to heal
The wounds of others I do not feel—
If my eyes are dry and I never weep,
How do I know when the hurt is deep—
If my heart is cold and it never bleeds,
How can I tell what my brother needs—
For when ears are deaf to the beggar's plea
And we close our eyes and refuse to see,
And we steel our hearts and harden our mind,
And we count it a weakness whenever we're kind,
We are no longer following *the Father's Way*
Or seeking His guidance from day to day—
For, without "crosses to carry" and "burdens to bear,"
We dance through a life that is frothy and fair,
And "chasing the rainbow" we have no desire
For "roads that are rough" and "realms that are higher"—
So spare me no heartache or sorrow, dear Lord,
For the heart that is hurt reaps the richest reward,
And God enters the heart that is broken with sorrow
As He opens the door to a *Brighter Tomorrow*,
For only through tears can we recognize
The suffering that lies in another's eyes.

God, Give Us "Drive" but Keep Us From Being "Driven"

There's a difference between "drive" and "driven"—
The one is selfish the other God-given—
For the "driven man" has but one goal,
Just worldly wealth and not "riches of soul,"
And daily he's spurred on to reach and attain
A higher position, more profit and gain,
Ambition and wealth become his great need
As daily he's "driven" by avarice and greed . . .
But most blessed are they who use their "drive"
To work with zeal so all men may survive,
For while they forfeit great personal gain
Their work and their zeal are never in vain . . .
For they contribute to the whole human race
And we cannot survive without growing in grace,
So help us, dear God, to choose between
The "driving force" that rules our routine
So we may make our purpose and goal
Not power and wealth but the growth of our soul . . .
And give us *strength* and *drive* and *desire*
To raise our standards and ethics higher
So all of Us and not *just a few*
May live on earth . . . *as You want Us to.*

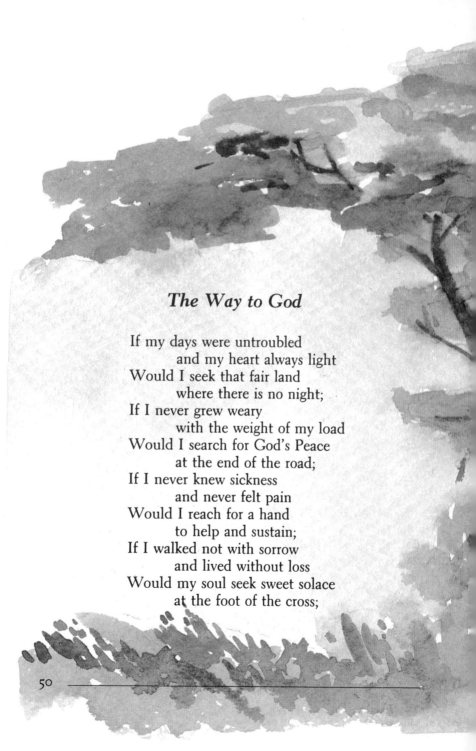

The Way to God

If my days were untroubled
     and my heart always light
Would I seek that fair land
     where there is no night;
If I never grew weary
     with the weight of my load
Would I search for God's Peace
     at the end of the road;
If I never knew sickness
     and never felt pain
Would I reach for a hand
     to help and sustain;
If I walked not with sorrow
     and lived without loss
Would my soul seek sweet solace
     at the foot of the cross;

If all I desired was mine
    day by day
Would I kneel before God
    and earnestly pray;
If God sent no "Winter"
    to freeze me with fear
Would I yearn for the warmth
    of "Spring" every year;
I ask myself this
    and the answer is plain—
If my life were all pleasure
    and I never knew pain
I'd seek God less often
    and need Him much less,
For God's sought more often
    in times of distress,
And no one knows God
    or sees Him as plain
As those who have met Him
    on "The Pathway of Pain.'

Prayers Can't Be Answered Unless They Are Prayed

Life without purpose
    is barren indeed—
There can't be a harvest
    unless you plant seed,
There can't be attainment
    unless there's a goal,
And man's but a robot
    unless there's a soul . . .
If we send no ships out,
    no ships will come in,
And unless there's a contest,
    nobody can win . . .
For games can't be won
    unless they are played,
And *Prayers* can't be *answered*
    unless they are *prayed* . . .
So whatever is wrong
    with your life today,
You'll find a solution
    if you kneel down and pray
Not just for pleasure,
    enjoyment, and health,
Not just for honors
    and prestige and wealth . . .
But *Pray for a Purpose*
    to *make life worth living.*
And *Pray for the Joy*
    of *unselfish giving,*
For *Great is your Gladness*
    and *Rich your Reward*
When you make your *Life's Purpose*
    the choice of the Lord.

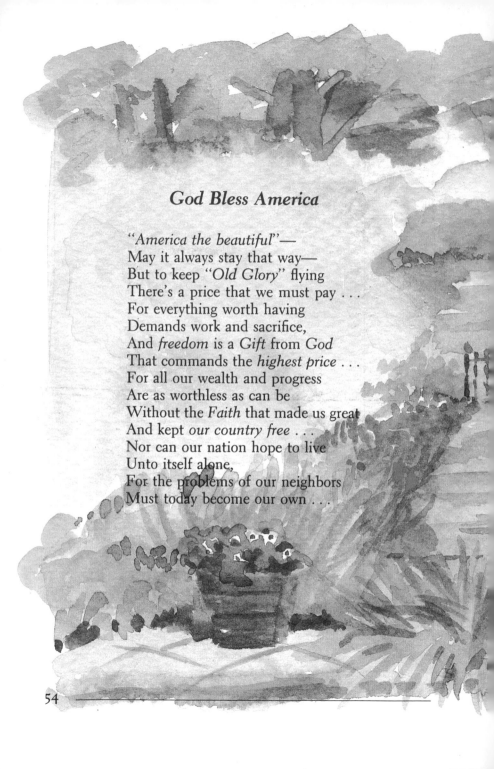

God Bless America

"*America the beautiful*"—
May it always stay that way—
But to keep "*Old Glory*" flying
There's a price that we must pay . . .
For everything worth having
Demands work and sacrifice,
And *freedom* is a *Gift* from *God*
That commands the *highest price* . . .
For all our wealth and progress
Are as worthless as can be
Without the *Faith* that made us great
And kept *our country free* . . .
Nor can our nation hope to live
Unto itself alone,
For the problems of our neighbors
Must today become our own . . .

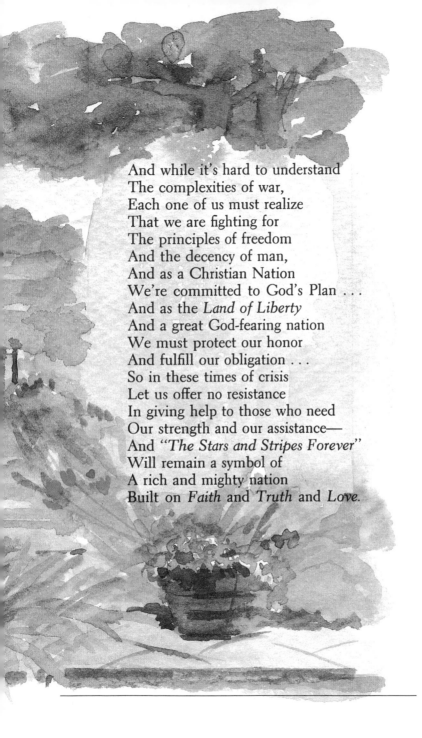

And while it's hard to understand
The complexities of war,
Each one of us must realize
That we are fighting for
The principles of freedom
And the decency of man,
And as a Christian Nation
We're committed to God's Plan . . .
And as the *Land of Liberty*
And a great God-fearing nation
We must protect our honor
And fulfill our obligation . . .
So in these times of crisis
Let us offer no resistance
In giving help to those who need
Our strength and our assistance—
And *"The Stars and Stripes Forever"*
Will remain a symbol of
A rich and mighty nation
Built on *Faith* and *Truth* and *Love.*

Count Your Gains and Not Your Losses

As we travel down life's busy road
Complaining of our heavy load,
We often think God's been unfair
And given us much more than our share
Of little daily irritations
And disappointing tribulations . . .
We're discontented with our lot
And all the "bad breaks" that we got,
We count our losses, not our gain,
And remember only tears and pain . . .
The good things we forget completely
When God looked down and blessed us sweetly,
Our troubles fill our every thought
We dwell upon lost goals we sought,
And wrapped up in our own despair
We have no time to see or share
Another's load that far outweighs
Our little problems and dismays . . .
And so we walk with head held low
And little do we guess or know
That someone near us on life's street
Is burdened deeply with defeat . . .
But if we'd but forget *our care*
And stop in sympathy to share
The burden that "our brother" carried,
Our mind and heart would be less harried
And we would feel our load was small,
In fact, *we carried no load at all.*

Everywhere Across the Land You See God's Face and Touch His Hand

Each time you look up in the sky
Or watch the fluffy clouds drift by,
Or feel the sunshine warm and bright,
Or watch the dark night turn to light,
Or hear a bluebird gayly sing,
Or see the winter turn to spring,
Or stop to pick a daffodil,
Or gather violets on some hill . . .
Or touch a leaf or see a tree,
It's all *God* whispering, *"This Is Me . . .*
And I am Faith and *I am Light*
And in Me there shall be no night."

God Knows Best

Our Father knows what's best for us,
So why should we complain—
We always want the sunshine,
But He knows there must be rain—
We love the sound of laughter
And the merriment of cheer,
But our hearts would lose their tenderness
If we never shed a tear . . .
Our Father tests us often
With suffering and with sorrow,
He tests us, not to punish us,
But to help us meet *tomorrow* . . .
For growing trees are strengthened
When they withstand the storm,
And the sharp cut of the chisel
Gives the marble grace and form . . .
God never hurts us needlessly,
And He never wastes our pain,
For every loss He sends to us
Is followed by rich gain . . .
And when we count the blessings
That God has so freely sent,
We will find no cause for murmuring
And no time to lament . . .
For Our Father loves His children,
And to Him all things are plain,
So He never sends us *pleasure*
When the *soul's deep need is pain* . . .
So whenever we are troubled,
And when everything goes wrong,
It is just God working in us
To make *our spirit strong.*

Blessings in Disguise Are Difficult to Recognize

God sends His "little angels"
     in many forms and guises,
They come as lovely miracles
     that God alone devises—
For He does nothing without purpose,
     everything's a perfect plan
To fulfill in bounteous measure
     all He ever promised man—
For every "little angel"
     with a body bent and broken,
Or a little mind retarded
     or little words unspoken,
Is just God's way of trying
     to reach and touch the hand

Of all who do not know Him
     and cannot understand
That often through an angel
     whose "wings will never fly"
The Lord is pointing out the way
     to His eternal sky
Where there will be no handicaps
     of body, soul, or mind,
And where all limitations
     will be dropped and left behind—
So accept these "little angels"
     as gifts from God above
And thank Him for this lesson
     in *Faith* and *Hope* and *Love.*

Birthdays Are a Gift From God

Where does *time* go in its endless flight—
Spring turns to fall and day to night,
And birthdays come and birthdays go
And where they go we do not know . . .
But God who planned our life on earth
And gave our mind and body birth
And then enclosed a living soul
With heaven as the spirit's goal
Has given man the gift of choice
To follow that small inner voice
That speaks to us from year to year
Reminding us we've naught to fear . . .
For *birthdays* are a *stepping-stone*
To endless joys as yet unknown,
So fill each day with happy things
And may your burdens all take wings
And fly away and leave behind
Great joy of heart and peace of mind . .   .
For *birthdays* are *the gateway* to
An *endless life of joy for you*
If you but pray from day to day
That He will show you the *Truth* and the *Way*.

My God Is No Stranger

I've never seen God,
      but I know how I feel . . .
It's people like *you*
      who make *Him "so real"* . . .
My God is no stranger,
      He's friendly and gay . . .
And *He* doesn't ask me
      to weep when I pray . . .
It seems that I pass *Him*
      so often each day . . .
In the faces of people
      I meet on my way . . .
He's the stars in the heaven,
      a smile on some face . . .
A leaf on a tree
      or a rose in a vase . . .
He's winter and autumn
      and summer and spring . . .
In short, *God Is Every*
      Real, Wonderful Thing . . .
I wish I might meet *Him*
      much more than I do . . .
I would if there were
      more people like you.

"Why Should He Die for Such as I"

In everything both great and small
We see the Hand of God in all,
And in the miracles of Spring
When *everywhere* in *everything*
His handiwork is all around
And every lovely sight and sound
Proclaims the God of earth and sky
I ask myself *"Just Who Am I"*
That God should send His only Son
That my salvation would be won
Upon a *cross* by a sinless man
To bring fulfillment to God's Plan—
For Jesus suffered, bled, and died
That sinners might be sanctified,
And to grant God's children *such as I*
Eternal life in that *Home on High*.

The Seasons of the Soul

Why am I cast down
      and despondently sad
When I long to be happy
      and joyous and glad?
Why is my heart heavy
      with unfathomable weight
As I try to escape
      this soul-saddened state?
I ask myself often—
      "What makes life this way,
Why is the song silenced
      in the heart that was gay?"
And then with God's help
      it all becomes clear,
The *Soul* has its *Seasons*
      just the same as the year—
I too must pass through
      life's autumn of dying,
A desolate period
      of heart-hurt and crying,
Followed by winter
      in whose frostbitten hand
My heart is as frozen
      as the snow-covered land—

Yes, man too must pass
      through the seasons God sends,
Content in the knowledge
      that everything ends,
And oh what a blessing
      to know there are reasons
And to find that our soul
      must, too, have its seasons—
Bounteous Seasons
      and *Barren Ones,* too,
Times for rejoicing
      and times to be blue,
But meeting these seasons
      of dark desolation
With strength that is born
      of anticipation
That comes from knowing
      that "autumn-time sadness"
Will surely be followed
      by a "Springtime of Gladness."

"I Am the Light of the World"

Oh, Father, up in heaven,
    We have wandered far away
From Jesus Christ, Our Saviour,
    Who arose on Easter Day . . .
And the promise of salvation
    That God gave us when Christ died
We have often vaguely questioned,
    Even doubted and denied . . .
We've forgotten why You sent us
    Jesus Christ Your Only Son,
And in arrogance, and ignorance—
    It's *Our Will,* not *Thine, Be Done* . . .
Oh, shed *Thy Light* upon us
    As Easter dawns this year,
And may we feel *The Presence*
    Of the *Risen Saviour* near . . .
And, God, in Thy great wisdom,
    Lead us in the way that's right,
And may *"The Darkness"* of this world
    Be conquered by *"Thy Light."*

Spring Song

"The earth is the Lord's
    and the fulness thereof"—
It speaks of His greatness
    and it sings of His love,
And the wonder and glory
    of the first Easter morn,
Like the first Christmas night
    when the Saviour was born,
Are blended together
    in symphonic splendor
And God with a voice
    that is gentle and tender
Speaks to all hearts
    attuned to His voice,
Bidding His listeners
    to gladly rejoice . . .
For He who was born
    to be crucified
Arose from the grave
    to be glorified . . .
And the birds in the trees
    and the flowers of Spring
All join in proclaiming
    this heavenly King.

In the Garden of Gethsemane

Before the dawn of Easter
  There came Gethsemane . . .
Before the Resurrection
  There were hours of agony . . .
For there can be no crown of stars
  Without a cross to bear,
And there is no salvation
  Without *Faith* and *Love* and *Prayer*,
And when we take our needs to God
  Let us pray as did His Son
That dark night in Gethsemane—
  "Thy Will, not Mine, Be Done."

"I Know That My Redeemer Liveth"

They asked me how I know it's true
That the Saviour lived and died . . .
And if I believe the story
That the Lord was crucified?
And I have so many answers
To prove His Holy Being,
Answers that are everywhere
Within the realm of seeing . . .
The leaves that fell at autumn
And were buried in the sod
Now budding on the tree boughs
To lift their arms to God . . .
The flowers that were covered
And entombed beneath the snow
Pushing through the "darkness"
To bid the Spring "hello" . . .
On every side Great Nature
Retells the Easter Story—
So who am I to question
"The Resurrection Glory?"

A Thankful Heart

Take nothing for granted,
  for whenever you do
The "joy of enjoying"
  is lessened for you—
For we rob our own lives
  much more than we know
When we fail to respond
  or in any way show
Our thanks for the blessings
  that daily are ours . . .
The warmth of the sun,
  the fragrance of flowers,
The beauty of twilight,
  the freshness of dawn,
The coolness of dew
  on a green velvet lawn,
The kind little deeds
  so thoughtfully done,
The favors of friends
  and the love that someone
Unselfishly gives us
  in a myriad of ways,
Expecting no payment
  and no words of praise—
Oh, great is our loss
  when we no longer find
A thankful response
  to things of this kind,
For the *joy of enjoying*
  and the *Fullness of living*
Are found in the heart
  that is filled with *Thanksgiving.*

Thank You, God, for Everything

Thank You, God, for everything—
  the big things and the small,
For "every good gift comes from God"—
  the giver of them all—
And all too often we accept
  without any thanks or praise
The gifts God sends as blessings
  each day in many ways,
And so at this *Thanksgiving time*
  we offer up a prayer
To thank You, God, for giving us
  a lot more than our share . . .
First, thank You for the little things
  that often come our way,
The things we take for granted
  but don't mention when we pray,

The unexpected courtesy,
the thoughtful, kindly deed,
A hand reached out to help us
in the time of sudden need . . .
Oh, make us more aware, dear God,
of little daily graces
That come to us with "sweet surprise"
from never-dreamed-of places—
Then, thank You for the *"Miracles"*
we are much too blind to see,
And give us new awareness
of our many gifts from Thee,
And help us to remember
that the *Key* to *Life* and *Living*
Is to make each prayer a *Prayer of Thanks*
and every day *Thanksgiving.*

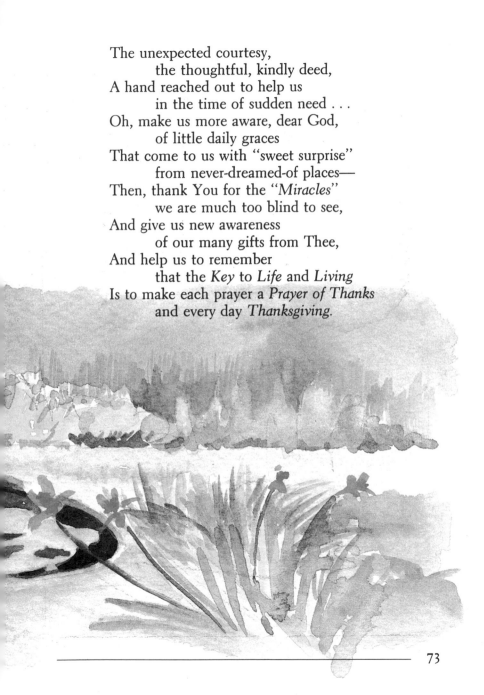

The Priceless Gift of Christmas

Now Christmas is a season
      for joy and merrymaking,
A time for gifts and presents,
      for giving and for taking . . .
A festive, friendly happy time
      when everyone is gay—
But have we ever really felt
      the *greatness of the day* . . .
For through the centuries the world
      has wandered far away
From the beauty and the meaning
      of the *Holy Christmas Day* . . .
For Christmas is a heavenly gift
      that only God can give,
It's ours just for the asking,
      for as long as we shall live . . .
It can't be bought or bartered,
      it can't be won or sold,
It doesn't cost a penny
      and it's worth far more than gold . . .
It isn't bright and gleaming
      for eager eyes to see,

It can't be wrapped in tinsel
        or placed beneath a tree . . .
It isn't soft and shimmering
        for reaching hands to touch,
Or some expensive luxury
        you've wanted very much . . .
For the *priceless Gift of Christmas*
        is meant just for the heart
And we receive it only
        when we become a part
Of the kingdom and the glory
        which is ours to freely take,
For God sent the Holy Christ Child
        at Christmas for our sake,
So man might come to know *Him*
        and feel *His Presence* near
And see the many miracles
        performed while *He* was here . . .
And this *priceless Gift of Christmas*
        is within the reach of all,
The rich, the poor, the young and old
        the greatest and the small . . .
So take *His Priceless Gift of Love,*
        reach out and you receive,
And the only payment that God asks,
        is just that *you believe.*

Let Us Pray on This Holy Christmas Day

What better time
And what better season,
What greater occasion
Or more wonderful reason
To kneel down in prayer
And lift our hands high
To the God of creation
Who made land and sky . . .
And, oh, what a privilege
As the New Year begins
To ask God to wipe out
Our errors and sins
And to know when we ask,
If we are sincere,
He will wipe our slate clean
As we start a New Year . . .
So at this glad season
When joy's everywhere,
Let us meet Our Redeemer
At the *Altar* of *Prayer.*

Faith Is a Mighty Fortress

We stand once more at the end of the year
With mixed emotions of *hope and fear,*
Hope for *the Peace* we long have sought,
Fear that *our hopes* will come to naught . . .
Unwilling to trust in the *Father's Will,*
We count on our logic and shallow skill
And, in our arrogance and pride,
Man is no longer satisfied
To place his confidence and love
With *Childlike Faith* in God above . . .
But tiny hands and tousled heads
That kneel in prayer by little beds
Are closer to the dear Lord's heart
And of His Kingdom more a part
Than we who search and never find
The answers to our questioning mind,
For faith in things we cannot see
Requires a child's simplicity . . .
Oh, Father, grant once more to men
A simple *Childlike Faith* again,
Forgetting *color, race,* and *creed*
And seeing only the heart's deep need . . .
For *Faith* alone can save man's soul
And lead him to a *higher goal,*
For there's but one unfailing course—
We win by *Faith* and *not* by *Force.*

After the Winter . . . God Sends the Spring

Springtime is a season
      Of Hope and Joy and Cheer,
There's beauty all around us
      To see and touch and hear . . .
So, no matter how downhearted
      And discouraged we may be,
New Hope is born when we behold
      Leaves budding on a tree . . .
Or when we see a timid flower
      Push through the frozen sod
And open wide in glad surprise
      Its petaled eyes to God . . .
For this is just God saying—
      "Lift up your eyes to Me,
And the bleakness of your spirit,
      Like the budding springtime tree,
Will lose its wintry darkness
    And your heavy heart will sing"—
For God never sends the Winter
      Without the Joy of Spring.

Out of My Life

*Little Lights and Shadows
from My Present and Past
as told to*
Donald T. Kauffman

Not long ago I received a letter from a man who asked me what I had done to "meet life successfully." As I tried to explain to him, I am a very ordinary person. I do not think of myself as a success, but as just another worker in God's vineyard. The phenomenal sale of my books and writings is not due to anything special about me or my way of living. It is a tribute to the wonderful goodness of God, not to me; at best, I am just an instrument for His message. This short account of my life has been written, at the publishers' request, not to publicize any "success secrets," but to show how completely God helps us solve our problems when we place ourselves completely in His mighty hands.

I was born in the bustling little town of Lorain, Ohio, on the shore of Lake Erie. Lorain is a busy lakeport; its steel mill is still one of the largest in the United States. Everyone in town was pretty much on an equal level socially, and my sister, Gertrude, and I had a very happy childhood.

My father, John A. Steiner, was a railroad engineer and a marvelous man. I never heard him swear once or lose his temper. My mother was high-spirited, but my father was always gentle and calm; he was just a very nice person. There was not an ounce of bias in him—he was as much at home with a Lake Erie fisherman as he would have been with the President. He loved to hunt, and he invited everyone from bankers to street-cleaners to come hunting with him.

Mother had an exceptional flair for making lovely clothes. Everyone said that I had the most beautiful clothes in the world, and for this all the credit goes to my dear mother. She was ambitious for her children; she wanted us to be well educated and to have the better things of life. But Papa and I felt we already had everything important, and we were content with life.

When I was sixteen and a senior in high school, the bottom dropped out of my life. Papa died in a flu epidemic. Although we were not destitute, I felt that I ought to do something to help my mother and younger sister, and I started thinking about a job.

I did not have to think about it long. I was offered work by the Lorain branch of the Ohio Public Service Company, first as a "pinch hitter" and then in other jobs for which I volunteered. Before long I was a director of public relations for Public Service and chairman of the women's committee on public relations for the National Electric Light Association (East Central Division).

One day I was asked to speak at an electric light convention at Cedar Point. When I got to the platform I thought to myself, *I don't really know how to start this, or what to say, or even how much.* I panicked a bit—then another thought came into my mind:

Your Father knows.

Then and there, in that split fraction of a second, I spoke to the God who means everything to me. I said, "I don't know what to do, Father—You tell me."

At that moment a wonderful feeling of assurance and confidence swept over me; I knew that my heavenly Father was answering.

There were a lot of businessmen at the convention. I picked out one who looked friendly and understanding and started talking to him and, from the response I could see in his face, I knew that what I wanted to say was getting across. Other faces started to respond, and when I finished, there was a long round of applause.

I have always spoken in public just as I would talk to someone in my living room. I never tried to make a name for myself, or to use big words, so I never had the tension and struggle of getting too involved with myself. I learned to let go and let God take control.

There were many things I was anxious to speak about. Women's rights were a constant topic while I was growing up; all my teachers had been suffragettes, and I firmly believed in the right and ability of women to win their own way in the world. I developed a number of lecture topics like "Blue Eyes or Gray Matter" and "Living and Working Enthusiastically."

I discovered the many men were ready and willing to listen to an enthusiastic presentation of these matters by a blonde young lady who knew how to appeal to their sense of humor as well as to their business interests and their sense of fair play.

I began receiving more and more invitations to speak. I addressed the American Electric Railway Convention (a very big thing at that time) in Washington, D. C. There I was photographed with President Calvin Coolidge. B. C. Forbes, publisher of *Forbes Magazine*, wrote me, "The place for you is not Lorain, Ohio, but some metropolitan city like New York where there is so much more room for doing big things." I had a number of statements of this kind printed in a circular, prepared a list of lecture topics, and started my own lecture circuit.

As long as I live, I'll remember the speech I made at the Statler Hotel in Buffalo, New York. (Mr. Storr, head of the Buffalo Board of Education, had read an interview with me in *Nation's Business* and had invited me to address a business luncheon at the Statler.)

When I arrived at the room where the luncheon was being held, everything was buzzing. I had never seen so many people in a room that size. I didn't know what Mr. Storr looked like, nor where I was to go; I guess I felt a little lost.

I approached a man at what looked like the head table and said, "I would like to talk to Mr. Storr."

The man replied, "You can't see him now. He's busy—he's hunting for the speaker."

I said, "I am the speaker."

The man was visibly upset. I thought he was going to collapse! He went away and returned soon with a large, imposing-looking gentleman who looked at me in such a way that, if I could have shriveled up under his gaze, I surely would have.

Finally he said, "There has been a mistake. We asked the woman who was photographed with President Coolidge to speak here. You are just a child!"

I *was* quite small and slender, and I was wearing a little gold two-piece dress with a purple toque pulled down over my forehead. At that time, dresses were *very* short, and Mr. Storr looked as if he thought I was a schoolgirl who had lost her way.

I said, "I'm it."

Mr. Storr tried awfully hard to be nice to me, but it was obviously a hardship. He said, "I don't think you can make yourself heard there. Have you ever talked to this many people?"

"Oh, yes," I said. "This room is really small compared to the Chamber of Commerce Hall where I spoke in Washington."

Mr. Storr said, "We've invited the whole John Larkin Company to this luncheon. John Larkin is here himself! I do hope you won't disappoint us."

What a way to build up confidence! But I asked my Father for help—as I have learned to do every time I make a speech or write a poem—and, at the end of my speech, Mr. Storr said, "I never would have believed you could do it." I must say that he did everything in his power to make up for the way he had greeted me. He escorted me to all the local attractions and sent me an enormous box of roses.

One evening I spoke to the Annual Clearinghouse Association of Bankers at the Dayton Country Club on the topic, "Do You Know Your Job or Do You *Love* Your Job?" The member delegated to meet the speaker was a tall, handsome young man named Franklin D. Rice. After the meeting, he asked me, "Would you like to go some place and have something to eat?" Many of those present kidded me about going out with the most eligible bachelor in Dayton, Ohio.

Franklin, I learned, had been a Lieutenant in the Air Force in World War I. And when I first met him, he was an officer with the Dayton Savings and Trust Company. He commuted a great deal to New York, and came from a family of outstanding ability and wealth. In a year we were married.

Everyone said that I was the luckiest girl in the world, and I had to agree. For our honeymoon Franklin had arranged a cruise through the Caribbean. We had a beautiful suite on an enormous luxury liner.

About a week after the cruise began, Franklin began getting daily cablegrams from his banking associates. The stock market was beginning to fall and the Great Depression was beginning. But Franklin never allowed himself to be anything but the perfect husband and host, gay and friendly to all aboard. Instead of panicking over Wall Street's crash, he followed the usually sound practice of buying while others were selling. He kept writing his bank to buy more and more stock.

For the next two years we lived more extravagantly than ever. Suspecting the truth, I wanted to let our servants go and return to work, but Franklin would not hear of it. "Do you want to advertise to the whole world that things are slipping?" he asked. "We must put up a good front no matter what happens."

Finally everything Franklin D. Rice had owned was gone. Then, one terrible gray morning, I woke up to find that Franklin was gone too. About all he left me was a note in which he had written:

Darling, The only thing I'm sorry about is that I never could give you all the things I meant to. I hope you believe that I really wanted to give them to you, and I could have given them to you before everything went. . . . You'll always go on. I only knew one world. I just can't go down and become a bum—I have to go out with the bands playing.

After my husband's tragic death, the officers of the Gibson Company asked me to work for them. When I asked what they wanted me to do, they said, "Just come and you'll find out."

The first thing they asked me to do was to make a general survey of the offices and tell them what to do to improve their greeting card business. Of course I had recommendations galore! I stylized the cards and formed various programs. Then the editor suddenly contracted pneumonia and died, and E. P. Gibson (the company's founder), his nephew J. R. Gibson, and the other officers asked me to become the new editor. Although I protested that I had never written a rhyme in my life, they said, "Just take the job until we get someone."

There is nothing about my life that I have really planned. I am a very definite believer in the philosophy of Christ: "Consider the lilies, how they grow." I think you have to be willing to work hard and do whatever job is put before you. I don't think you can just sit down and say, "I don't want that because I want to be the head of it all." I have never been the head of anything. I always start out trying to do the job I have been given—and I always see a lot more in the job than what it had when I began it.

Still, *God's* plan is wonderful. And His timing is perfect. I always leaned toward a clear expression of faith in the cards I produced; I don't believe in keeping inside what you believe about God. He is no one to be ashamed of! But it never became possible for my poems to be published until a few years ago. I am convinced that if they had been published when I wanted them to be, they would not have found ready acceptance. *Now* is the time the world so desperately needs these messages of faith and inspiration, and people would not have responded to them previously, as they do today. The world is in such turmoil now that a great many men and women and young people are ready to listen to the message.

Millions of my poems have now been printed, and the first compilation of them ever published has sold more than 700,000 copies in less than seven years. And its seventh printing sells just as well as the newest volume off the press.

As many of my readers know, Lawrence Welk selected my poem "The Priceless Gift of Christmas" for reading on his television show, and this produced thousands of new customers for my work. That reading by Aladdin was a marvelous answer to prayer, as I pointed out in my poem "How It All Happened."

Six years ago on *The Lawrence Welk Show*
An artist whom so many folks know
Received a card with a Christmas verse
That spoke of *The Holy Christ Child's Birth*—
And for some reason it caught his eye,
And I doubt today that he even knows *Why*.
For the reader and writer had never met
But the writer is one who will never forget
The joyous amazement and rapt surprise

When out of the starlit Christmas skies
Across the country from shore to shore
An unknown verse never heard before
Was heard by millions of listening ears,
And the writer's dream of many years
Was answered by God in a wonderful way,
And from that night to this present day
Aladdin still reads with his magic touch
The verses that people have liked so much—
And while it may look like a happenstance,
Or something born of a lucky chance,
The writer is sure that God drew the plan
And put it into the hands of man.
And, Aladdin,
      one of *the Lawrence Welk band,*
Just carried out what the Lord had planned—
For I had prayed for many long years
Through disappointments and often tears
To find, without attempts to preach,
A way that I could somehow reach
Responsive hearts . . . much like *my own*
And tell them *"No One Walks Alone"*—
But little did I guess or know
My prayer would be answered on
      The Lawrence Welk Show,
For since *"The Priceless Gift"* was aired,
Through *Aladdin's voice* I've often shared
All the verses between these covers.
And through the years there may be others
That I can share with folks like you
For there's *nothing* I would rather do—
And this is *the story* of *"How It Began"*
Six years ago with "The Music Man."

A year later my poem "The Praying Hands" was read on the Welk show. Then, early in 1962, John Glenn became the first American to orbit the earth, and his remarkable testimony of faith in God inspired and delighted millions who had been thrilled by his historic flight. I composed a poem of tribute to John's mother, which was read by Aladdin that Mother's Day. John Glenn's mother wrote me:

> I received your lovely poem . . . I am so thrilled by it, I hardly know how to write to you. It is beautiful . . . I plan to have the copy you sent to me framed, and keep it always.

From all over the world I received wonderful letters about my poems. A delegate to the United Nations took one of my books back to Bombay, and his secretary read it. She wrote me a glowing letter of appreciation, adding:

> At present there is a problem about our home which I (and my parents) are most worried about and we all are most earnestly praying about it. At first, I guess, worry was a block, which made me, too, have a feeling that my prayers were not getting through. Now, even though the outcome is not evident, I am knowing, as you so well put it, "No matter in what guise or disguise things come to us, they are sent for our good from Our Father."
>
> I just thought I would let you know how very much your letters and poems help me.

A woman in Minnesota wrote:

> You are causing people to pause, weigh values, and turn to the God who made us, when we need to be sustained—when our "original batteries" need recharging!

A secretary wrote of my book *Just for You:*

By the time I finished reading it, I felt as if I could move mountains, or withstand one falling on me. I wish everyone had the opportunity to read this certainly unforgettable book.

A Kentucky lady wrote:

In the past year I have read any and all of your poems I could get ahold of. Without you and your beautiful poetry to remind me constantly of God's love, I don't know where I would be—perhaps even dead—yes, even killed by my own hand. Your beautiful poetry has reminded me every hour of every day how much God cares.

You see, I have leukemia, and have a year—perhaps two—to live. And all of a sudden I was terribly frightened. I shouldn't be, I know—God was close—He had always been—and yet I felt that all of a sudden He had forgotten me.

Then—Helen Steiner Rice—I read "The End of the Road Is But a Bend in the Road," and all of a sudden I felt better. I read every poem of yours that I could get ahold of, and with each one I felt better until I'm not afraid anymore—I am closer to God than ever before, and when my time comes—I'm ready.

Another person wrote me about a cousin who was in prison:

This man had done a wrong and is paying for it at this time at the Indiana State Prison. He happens to be a cousin of mine. Since I believe in the human race I write to this man and try to encourage him. And believe you me he needs all the encouragement he can get. You may be interested to know that one way I have for doing this is to buy the most beautiful verses by Helen Steiner Rice that I can find. Not only does he get a lot of good and encouragement from these but I read and reread them myself before I send them and they give me the special lift that we all need every now and then.

I spend a lot of time replying to letters like these. Probably seventy-five percent of them are from people in small towns or villages, or from lonely dwellers on prairies or in apartments. A dear little grandmother wrote me that after buying my book *Just for You* she bought seven copies for her children, and then four copies for other relatives, and then six more to give to friends! She said:

> I will never get tired of reading your poems. They have brought me closer to God and have renewed my faith and given me new hope and love. I only pray every night that God will bless you with lots of good health so you can keep on writing forever and doing His work.

God does bless me with *countless* blessings. But I don't want anyone to think that I'm always happy and on top of the world. Sometimes I feel like an empty, dried-out corn husk. But, as Jimmie Davis sings, "You've got to keep on walking." Many days I say to my marvelously efficient secretary, "Mary Jo, today I feel as flat and drained out as though a ten-ton truck just ran over me. But we've got to keep going, because if we don't, we're not going to keep up with the schedule!"

Each morning before I go to my office I say this little prayer:

> Bless me, heavenly Father,
>   forgive my erring ways,
> Grant me strength to serve Thee,
>   put purpose in my days . . .
> Give me understanding
>   enough to make me kind
> So I may judge all people
>   with my heart and not my mind . . .
> And teach me to be patient
>   in everything I do,
> Content to trust Your wisdom
>   and to follow after You . . .
> And help me when I falter
>   and hear me when I pray
> And receive me in *Thy Kingdom*
>   to dwell with Thee some day.

Many times, during the day, I find occasion to repeat two of the lines: "Teach me to be *patient*" and *"Help me when I falter!"*

As I think back over the wonderful years I have enjoyed, I truly feel that many people are not really living—that somehow they miss the beauty and joy and goodness that God has put all around them. If my poems do anything, I believe they help people find the satisfaction of living life to its fullest. God's gifts are all around us, but so many people who receive them don't seem to be aware of them, and sometimes it seems to me that they never fully enjoy them.

Living is like breathing. I want to breathe deep so I can live! And it's possible to miss the joy of filling our lungs with fresh clean air, as well as the joy of living each moment to its fullest.

My own life has overflowed with happiness. And God has taught me the blessed secret of finding His purposes in even tragically black moments. Even the events that are unhappiest pass away and turn into things that are really wonderful. I can't waste my time thinking about things that are sad, because there are so many good things in life. Why should I dwell on the things that would only make me unhappy?

Whenever anyone thanks me for one of my books or poems, I have to give all the credit to God. I don't have much to do with these poems, really. Everything I write is borrowed—it's from God, and from His age-old wisdom. I'm only an instrument for getting His message into people's lives. God gives me the ability to put it down, then He directs the traffic and gets my verse into the hands and hearts of people who find their own souls reflected in what I write.

As I said on one interview show, I have the best material in the world to work with, so nothing can compete with it! How can anyone do better than repeat the simple old words of faith and hope and kindness and love? Everything in the world may change, but these things are always valid.

Sometimes cynical people ask me what proof I have of these invisible realities I write about. What more proof could there be than what God puts all around us? Spiritual reality is like the air. You can't see it, but you can feel it, you know it is there and you couldn't live without it. I like to get up early in the morning and enjoy the wonderful songs of the birds and the smell of the flowers and trees. Then, when I walk into my office, I ask,

Who but God could make the day
And gently tuck the night away?

At times, I must confess, I have wondered why I had to lose my husband, Franklin, so tragically, after just the two short years we had together. Only in the last three or four years have I been sure why it was permitted to happen as it did.

The night before Franklin and I were married, I told the story of a young girl who stood at the edge of a field of waving corn—a beautiful field, where every stalk was tall and green and luxuriant and every ear was perfect. And the farther the girl could see into the field, the larger the ears became.

A genie told the girl, "If you walk through this field, I will reward you with a gift in proportion to the size of the ear you select. There is only one restriction. You must start right where you are standing, and you may go through the field only once. You may not retrace your steps. The ear of corn you bring out will determine the reward you will receive on the other side of the field."

The girl was supremely happy as she started into the field. Carelessly she trod on many of the stalks, thinking to herself: *I won't take any of these, for in the center of the field are the most perfect ears of all. I want the biggest reward I can get.*

The girl ran on and on, intent on finding the largest ear in the field. Suddenly she realized that the corn stalks were getting smaller and thinner; she was nearing the far edge of the field. In desperation, she looked for a good ear, but she could not bring herself to pick any of those in sight. She kept thinking, *There's got to be another big ear before the end.* But there was not. She came out of the field empty-handed.

I realize now, more surely than ever before, that *things* can never bring happiness. So many people always look for something bigger and better, and as soon as they get one thing, they set their hearts on another. Happiness is, for them, a mink coat or a Cadillac—something big, something splashy. If someone shakes hands with them and says "God bless you," sincerely, they fail to realize that they have just received one of the greatest gifts there is.

If you take the love and friendship and the "God bless you's" that come your way, you have everything. The person who gets the mink coat receives nothing really worthwhile or lasting. But the true gifts of God can never be lost.

As this book nears completion, another summer of riot and bloodshed is drawing near. I have just driven through the area of Cincinnati that was ravaged and burned in a recent uprising. I looked with unbelief at the devastation and destruction so savagely done by the "hand of evil," which is spreading across our country like a killing blight, and I am stunned with sadness.

There is so little that words can say at a time like this. For in these dark hours, the heart is overwhelmed with a heaviness that brings us to a closer awareness of Christ's Cross. As I write, Good Friday approaches, and we can almost feel that we are walking with the Saviour to our Calvary. This is not a time for words, it is a time for meditation, for our own Gethsemane.

Surely, only love can heal the sick, tired world. But God stands ready through His Son to turn this Cross into a Crown—if we will but let Him warm our cold hearts with His love.

I firmly believe that,

Great is the power
of might and mind,
But Only Love
Can Make Us Kind . . .
And all we are
or hope to be
is empty pride
and vanity . . .
if love is not
a part of all,
The Greatest Man
Is Very Small!

Yes,

Love is the language every heart speaks
And Love is the answer to all that man seeks.

Every one of my books begins with my own "Foreword" and ends with "My Thanks." I do not want this book to be any different, for how well I know that everything I have ever done is truly a gift from God. In His love I pass these gifts on from my heart to yours.

My Thanks!

People everywhere in life
  from every walk and station,
From every town and city
  and every state and nation
Have given me so many things
  intangible and dear,
I couldn't begin to count them all
  or even make them clear . . .
I only know I owe so much
  to people everywhere
And when I put my thoughts in verse
  it's just a way to share
The musings of a thankful heart,
  a heart much like your own,
For nothing that I think or write
  is mine and mine alone . . .
So if you found some beauty
  in any word or line,
It's just "Your Soul's Reflection"
  in "Proximity with Mine."

HELEN STEINER RICE